THE MEDIEVAL VILLAGE

THEN AND THERE SERIES

GENERAL EDITOR

MARJORIE REEVES, M.A., Ph.D.

The Medieval Village

MARJORIE REEVES, M.A., Ph.D.

Illustrated from contemporary sources by

F. E. GORNIOT

LONGMANS

LONGMANS, GREEN AND CO LTD
London and Harlow
Associated companies, branches and representatives
throughout the world

First published 1954
Second impression 1954
Third impression 1955
Fourth impression 1958
Fifth impression 1959
Sixth impression 1960
Seventh impression 1962
Eighth impression 1965
Ninth impression 1966
Tenth impression 1968

Printed in Hong Kong by Peninsula Press Ltd.

CONTENTS

TO THE READER

Every fact in this book comes from some record written at the time the book is describing; nothing has been invented in these pages, which seek to be a true record of the life and thought of people who themselves lived in medieval villages. What they wrote are original sources to which historians have to go back for their information. If you want to write a historical play or novel, see if you too can take your detail exactly and accurately from original sources.

In the same way every picture in this book is based on a drawing made by someone who lived then and there. You will find out more about these original sources and pictures by reading pages 83 and 84.

By studying what people said in word and picture about themselves, you will come to feel at home in one ' patch ' of the history of the past and really live with the group of people as they thought and worked. And gradually you will be able to fill in more patches of history.

The sources of the pictures include *The Luttrell Psalter*, *The Gorleston Psalter* and *Queen Mary's Psalter*, which are in the British Museum, and *The Romance of Alexander*, which is in the Bodleian Library, Oxford. The illustration on p. 75 is part of the Court Roll of Letcombe Regis, in the Public Record Office (P.R.O. Court Roll (S.C.2.), 154/35), and is reproduced from *The Manor and Manorial Records* by Nathaniel J. Hone by permission of Messrs. Methuen & Co., Ltd.

The Editors acknowledge with thanks the help of Mrs. J. G. S. Ward, Ph.D., in collecting some of the material for this book.

I WONDER whether you live in a town or a village. Do you see green fields out of your windows? Do you grow any of your own food to eat? Wherever you live, I expect your mother buys most of your food in the shops. Most of us would go very hungry if there were no food to buy in shops.

Six hundred and fifty years ago people lived usually in villages or quite small towns with fields close round them, and they grew most of their own food in those fields. This book is about one of these villages somewhere in the middle of England. I am going to call it Westwood. Perhaps your own town or village was very much like this one in those days. When you have read the book you can decide for yourself whether you would rather be living then or now.

To decide that, you will want to know lots of things about the village six hundred and fifty years ago. I have made a list of the questions I think you would ask, but you can make your own list as well.

What did the village look like?
What sort of houses did the people live in?
What were their clothes like?
What did they have to eat?
What did they do all day?
Did they have any fun and games?
Were there any thieves and were they ever caught?

Now, if you read on, I hope you will find the answers to these questions. Sometimes you will find a word written like *this*. You can find the meaning of these words from the Glossary on page 88.

WHAT THE VILLAGE LOOKED LIKE

The best way to see the whole of a place quickly today is to go up in an aeroplane and take a photograph. The best way to have seen the village of Westwood six hundred and fifty years ago would have been to climb to the top of one of the tall trees in the churchyard and draw a plan of what you saw. There it is on the opposite page.

First of all, find the stream in the plan. From the treetop it looks like a silver-blue thread in the grass. If there were no stream or well here, there would be no village. Why is this stream so important?

Now look at the houses, each one in its own small yard, and the large manor-house with barns round it. The lord and lady of the manor are Sir William de Cleverley and Lady Blanche, his wife.

Can you find the three great *arable* fields? (Remember to look up the word *arable*, if you don't know what it means.) The great East Field is bright green at the moment, for the young wheat is growing there. The South Field is full of barley. But the third big field, the West Field, is quite brown. Nothing is planted there because it is lying *fallow*, that is, having a rest for a year. (Why do the villagers leave it fallow?

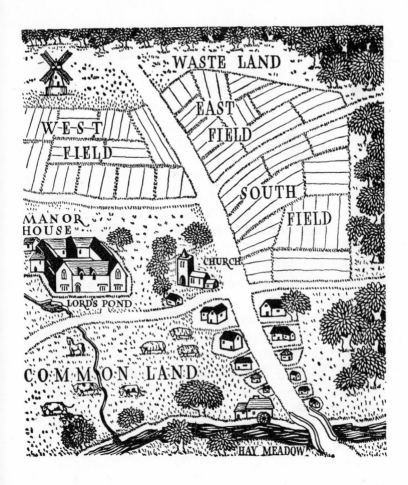

Will the same field be fallow next year ?) You will notice that the big fields are divided into strips of land by little grass paths. Most of the families in the village have a number of strips scattered about in each field, and Sir William also has his own strips in the same fields. His part of the land is called the *demesne*. Do you think it is a good idea to have your land in scattered strips ? What difficulties might arise ?

Notice the common land. Can you think what use the villagers will make of all this grassland ? You can see the cattle grazing there. The cowherd and shepherd are probably lying under a tree watching the animals (or sleeping !). Why are the sheep and the cattle so important ? Down by the stream the little goose-girl is paddling as she guards the geese and ducks. Near the stream, where the ground is damp, the grass is growing tall and thick in the hay-meadow, and close by you can see the watermill, with its big wheel turning round and round in the water as it grinds corn. It belongs to Sir William. He has two mills, but the other is a windmill. Why did he build the windmill on top of the hill ?

If you look further away still, beyond the fields and the cattle, you will see dark woods nearly all round the village. Somewhere under those trees the pigs are grunting as they root about for acorns. Further still inside the woods, far away in their own secret places, the wild deer hide. And who knows what you might find hiding there, and what adventures you might have in that dark forest ?

HOUSES OUTSIDE AND INSIDE

Most of the village people are called *villeins*. The lord of the manor gives each villein space for a house and garden, strips of land in the arable fields and a share in the hay-meadow and in the common land and wood-land. Instead of paying rent, each villein works on certain days for the lord of the manor and also gives him various things, like eggs at Christmas and a lamb at Easter.

How would you like to build your own house? John the villein built his own house with the help of his neighbours. He had no bricks or stones, but the lord let him cut down trees in the forest to make a house of timber. First he felled a tree. To build the house he

made a frame-work of timber, filled in the spaces with a lattice-work of thin wood, and plastered this all over with a mixture of mud and chopped straw. In this way he made a *wattle and daub wall*. Last of all he thatched the roof with straw. Do you think his house was water-tight? Think of all the differences you can between John the villein's house and your own.

Do you notice that John's house has no chimney? Inside there is a flat stone for a fire in the middle of the room and a smokehole in the roof above it. You can think for yourself why this is not as good as a fireplace and chimney. Margaret, John's wife, has to cook indoors in winter time but you can guess what happens, and why she cooks out of doors when she can. The window has no glass in it because nobody in the village knows how to make glass. So John has made wooden shutters for his window, and I leave you to think how inconvenient these are! There is no gas or electricity in this house. Why not?

The house has two rooms. In one room John keeps his tools and all the animals sleep by night. In the other room John and all his family live and sleep, for there is no upstairs at all. John has coloured his walls with a blue wash made from a plant called liverwort. He .has a wooden table, some three-legged stools, a log against the wall for the children's seat, and a bed like a big wooden box. That does not seem much furniture, but remember that John made every bit of it himself. The floor is just mud, stamped down very hard and firm. You will not find any cupboards for putting away your clothes or keeping the food. All the clothes go in one big wooden chest, and most of the food is kept in baskets. In one corner there is a wooden trough in which Margaret makes the bread. By it is an iron *cauldron*. Margaret uses the cauldron for a great many things. She cooks the dinner, washes the clothes, and even baths the baby in it! On the table are wooden plates and cups and a clay

jug. John made them all. The only thing Margaret had to buy was her iron cauldron, and for that she could not go to a shop, but had to wait till a travelling *pedlar* came round selling the things which the village folk could not make for themselves.

If you look up into the dark roof of John's home you will see big pieces of bacon and strings of fish hanging by the smokehole to get smoked ready for eating in the winter. A tiny door leads into a little wooden shed. If you go in there you must be careful not to fall into the great tub of salt water in which Margaret is pickling pork for the winter. When the animals are in the other room you can hear them grunting through the wooden wall, but today the place is empty except for a hen or two and a lazy old pig. John's tools are in one corner.

He has a hoe, a spade, an axe, a wooden bucket, a *sickle*, a *flail*, and of course his bows and arrows. If you don't know what all these are for, you will find out later on in this book.

Margaret has not got much housework to do, but other things take time. For one thing, nobody in the village has water brought to the house by pipes. There is one deep well in the middle of the village where everyone goes to draw water. So you see, John and Margaret go out of doors to get their water and cook their dinner. Here is Margaret at the well, while John blows up her fire with a big pair of bellows :

Have you ever seen anyone winding up a bucket of water like this ?

Now look at the house next to John's. This is much smaller and poorer, and only has a tiny garden.

This belongs to a poor cottager named Roger Mouse, who only has a very few strips of land from the lord. He has not got to do as much work for the lord as John, but he is so poor that in his spare time he will work for John or for other villagers if they will pay him a few pennies a day. He had nothing but mud, straw and some wood to build his house. So first he built a wall of mud about as high as your desk, and put straw along the top, and left it to dry. Then he built another piece on top and left that to dry. And so he went on until it was high enough to put a thatched roof of straw on. There is only one room in Roger's house, where he and his family and his cows and pigs and hens all live together.

Most of the houses in the village belong either to villeins like John or cottagers like Roger. The villeins have more strips of land but they do more work for the lord. Some have special jobs, like John Cherryman— the lord's ploughman, Gilbert the swineherd, Bray the miller, Peter Chaffinch the cowherd. Adam the bee-keeper, old William the shepherd, and Robert Pinchum the *hayward*. You will be reading about some of these later on.

Now let us look at a house which is bigger and grander than the rest. What differences do you notice between this and John's house?

It belongs to an important man in the village, Henry of Combe, the lord's *bailiff*, who looks after the farming of the lord's land. He is richer than the others and so has been able to buy bricks and tiles for his house. He has actually copied the latest fashion and made a chimney. Inside he has one high room called the hall, and a little staircase leading up to a small room called the bower. He is very proud of his house. Only one or two other people in Westwood are as rich as Henry. They are called free-holders, because they have more freedom to do what they like with their land than the villeins have.

The next house has a special sign. Look at it !

This sign means that Meg Merry brews ale from barley
and sells it there. She has to be very careful to brew it
properly. One day she mixed the ale with water and
got into trouble with the manor court. She is so poor
that they let her off paying a fine, but she won't dare do it
again.

There are no shops in this village six hundred and
fifty years ago, but next to the ale house is the blacksmith's
forge, like a black cave with a great red eye of fire shining
at the back of it. Sparks fly up in showers and you can
hear the sound of a sharp " ting, ting," as the blacksmith
beats out the white-hot iron on the anvil. His boy
blows up the fire with a large pair of bellows. It's a
nice warm job ! The blacksmith is a very important
person in the village. Make a list for yourself of all the
different tools he has to make and mend. In return for
his work he gets some land from the lord, and various

presents, such as a horse-skin to make his bellows, or butter to grease them, or a lamb or a cheese.

At the top of the village is the Church with dark yew trees round it. It is a very new Church. In fact it has not yet been finished. The villagers all joined together to rebuild it because their old one was too small. Everyone either helped or gave something. They have made tall pointed windows and a door with a porch and a tower with bells in it. Close by, in a house like the bailiff's, lives the Rector of the Church. He has some land and animals of his own, and besides this he lives on the presents which the people give him of corn, hens and so on ; these presents are called *tithes*.

Now we have visited most of the buildings except the manor house, which you will see later. I expect you will think of many things in your own town or village which we have not found in Westwood.

HERE COME THE PEOPLE

From the next three pictures, you will find out how the villagers dress. Here are John and Margaret coming home from work in the fields :

Notice John's tunic, leather boots with soft soles, and leather gloves. Why do you think he wears a cloth hood under his felt hat? Margaret's dress is of wool with a *girdle* round her waist and a linen cloth called a *wimple* round her head. How would you like to work in these clothes?

Here are some folk dressed for winter :

Sometimes they wear thick stockings, called *hose*, instead of boots. Shepherds often have special rabbit-skin hoods made with the fur inside, for they have to sleep out of doors on cold nights. In summer many people wear big straw hats in the field and go barefoot.

Here are some of the children in the village :

Do you think they wear sensible clothes ?

John and Margaret have four children, named William, Thomas, John and Joan. Thomas is rather a terror. He is a very good shot with his catapult and will go round potting at anything he sees. He hit old mother Hopper's sow slap on the snout and it squealed so much that its mistress came rushing out and beat him. Worse still, he saw Nicholas Croke's fine peacock strutting in the sun one day, and before he had stopped to think, he had hit and killed the poor bird. Then there was a fine row, for Nicholas is *Reeve* of the village and he is very proud of his peacock. Thomas was fined threepence in the manor court for that.

There is no school in the village, but sometimes the Rector has all the children in Church to teach them about the Bible. They have lots of other things to learn which are not taught in school, for even when they are very small they have to take their share of work. First, they learn to look after the hens and geese, find acorns and nuts, and draw water of the well. William is old enough now to learn how to plough and sow. When the roof of their house is getting thin, he can help his father thatch it again. Thomas is often sent to scare the black rooks off the corn. You can guess why. John and Joan are small but they can pick rushes by the stream to make rushlights. They help their mother peel these, dip them in hot grease or beeswax and hang them up to dry. Rushlights are saved for the dark wintertime. Can you think of other things the children will learn to do? Do you think their lessons are very different from yours?

Sometimes Margaret takes the children out to pick different plants that are good for medicine or cooking. She teaches them which leaves to boil to make a drink good for someone with a fever, and how a cowslip drink will make a sick person sleep, and many other things. You see, there is no doctor in the village. Margaret is the family doctor, though if someone is very ill Lady Blanche from the Manor House will try to cure them with some special medicines she knows how to make.

The women have to work hard to keep their families in clothes. They cannot go and buy cloth in the shops, so they have to start right at the beginning with the wool as it comes off the sheep's back. When the men bring it in, it is all in a dirty tangled mass. So first they scrub and beat it clean.   Now you can see what they do next :

Do you see them combing it out and spinning (or twisting) the wool into one long thread ?   To spin they put a large mass of wool on to a stick called a *distaff*, tie a *spindle* (or top) to an end of wool, and then set the spindle spinning so that the wool is pulled out into one long twisted thread.   Today we spin our thread very differently.   Can you find out how ?   It takes these women a long time to spin enough thread to make a piece of cloth, and whenever they have no other work to do you will find them spinning.   Margaret always seems to have her distaff tucked under her arm, and when the women sit gossiping in the sun they are spinning all the time.   Sometimes they quarrel !   One day Agnes, who is a bad old gossip, said that Alice, the wife of Walter Mustard, had taken one of her sheets which was drying on the hedge to make a shirt for her husband.

Alice said she didn't, and then they flew at each other with their distaffs and there would have been a proper fight if Walter had not come along and separated them. Look at them ! You will hear about Agnes's bad tongue again.

Look back at the picture of the women at work and find out how the thread is woven into cloth on a loom. I wonder if you have learnt to weave yet ? When Margaret has woven her piece of cloth she decides what colour she will dye it. She gets moss or the lichen which grows on trees or onion skins or berries. She makes her dye from these, and then she boils her cloth in the dye until it is the colour she wants—brown, red, green, blue or yellow. Then, when she had stretched and dried it in the sun, she is ready at last to make a new tunic for John or one of the children. If you can get a bit of sheep's wool, you can try spinning, weaving and dying for yourself.

The women also weave linen for their wimples. Find out for yourself where they get the linen thread from. Sometimes they make rough sack-cloth out of *hemp* or the threads in nettles. John makes all the boots for his family. He uses cow-skin which he *tans* to make good soft leather. Then he makes soft boots for all the family. As all these clothes have to be made at home, no one gets many new ones. John usually has one new tunic in the year, two shirts, one pair of hose, and one pair of boots. Tunics last a long time and get well patched. Old John the shepherd boasts that his hood and tunic are twelve years old !

FOOD AND DRINK

How would you like to go to work without any breakfast and have two meals a day ? That is what John does. As soon as it is light in the morning the village gets busy. They have no clocks, so how do you think they know the time ? Of course a real lazybones like John Gotobed stays in bed half the morning, but then his strips are full of weeds ! Nearly everyone is up by 6 o'clock in summer—turning out the animals, *yoking* the oxen, and getting off to the fields. Sometimes John has a bit of bread and a mug of ale, but nothing else.

At 10 o'clock in the morning everyone comes trooping back with huge appetites for dinner. This is their big meal ! John and his family sit on stools round the wooden table. There is no tablecloth, and they use their fingers for spoons and forks. The big clay jug has ale in it, and they have wooden plates and cups. In summer, when there is plenty to eat, they have fresh meat like beef or mutton for dinner, with bread and cheese and butter. On Fridays everyone eats fish—sometimes pickled herrings or cockles and mussels, but generally fish out of their own streams. In winter food is scarce. There is not much hay to keep the cattle alive and so the villagers have to kill nearly all their cows and pigs and salt the meat. Then they eat salt meat and bacon until they are tired of it. Often the corn does not last out the winter either, and they have to make coarse brown bread out of rye or oats or peas and beans. If they finish up everything else there are always cabbages and onions and parsley from the garden to eat, but these are not very filling !

After dinner everyone goes to work again until 4 o'clock when it is suppertime. (There is no teatime because no one knows that there is such a thing as tea.) For supper there is bacon and bread and cheese, with ale again to drink, or sometimes oatcake and *pottage*, which is soup with vegetables in it. Do you think these meals sound very dull ? You will think of many things to eat and drink that John the villein has never heard of, but remember that John and his family have to grow all their own food for themselves.

Instead of washing up after supper all the plates are scrubbed with grass and scraped with a knife. John goes out again to feed the animals and make them comfortable for the night. As soon as it is dark, people go to bed, for rushlights give a very feeble light, and anyway they are precious. They pull out straw mattresses and spread them on the floor, and get the blankets out of the chest. The children sleep on these and their father and mother in the box bed. Not many people bother with sheets, and a log does quite well for a pillow. Soon the whole family is asleep while next door the pigs grunt now and again or a cow bumps against the thin wooden wall.

THIEVES BY NIGHT

One night when everyone lay deep in sleep, someone came stealthily into the house of Peter Chaffinch. It was easy to do this because there was no lock and key to the door. Before Peter and his wife Alice could stir, the man had seized and tightly bound them with cords so that they had no power to cry out or to help themselves. Then the thief ransacked the house, laying hands on all the bread and corn, and carrying off their one warm bed coverlet, a sheet and towel, and Peter's best clothes. As he fled poor Peter caught a glimpse of him in the moonlight and thought it was Adam Doget. Peter and Alice could not stir, and there they lay, stiff and cramped, till daybreak when the neighbours came to call them for ploughing. And when they saw them through the open door lying bound on the bed, the neighbours raised the *hue and cry* : " Thief ! Thief ! "

Then Peter told them to go after Adam Doget, so they went through the village looking for him until they came to the house of Simon le Fox, and there they found Adam hiding. But the stolen property was nowhere to be found, and Adam denied that he had ever been near John's house. Simon, too, swore that Adam had slept in his house all night. It was only Peter's word against Adam's, and so the dispute had to wait to be settled in the manor court. You will see later on in this book what happened.

THE LORD AND LADY OF THE MANOR

Here are Sir William de Cleverley and Lady Blanche with their three children, William (aged 10), Thomas (aged 8) and Eleanor (aged 3). Look carefully at their clothes.

Here is the Manor House, where they live:

The Manor House

Sir William has several different manors, and the family moves round from one to another, living quite a long time in each manor house. They like coming to Westwood because Sir William's father built a nice new manor house here which is warmer and more comfortable than the other old draughty ones. This one is built of stone and has a high wall all round and a strong gate, for armed bands of men still sometimes attack manor houses. Inside the gate, there is an open space to cross and then you enter through a porch into a dark passage, called the *screens*. On the right, two doors lead into the great hall. This is the centre of the whole house.

THE HALL EMPTY OF FURNITURE

It is 35 feet long, 30 feet wide, and 22 feet high. Can you measure your own classroom and find out how much bigger this hall is ? It is rather dark inside, but you can see right up into the high, pointed roof built of timber.

The servants eat their meals at two long *trestle-tables* running down the hall and Sir William and his family at the high table placed across the far end. In the middle of the hall there is a great brick hearth with a large fire of logs blazing on it, and a smoke hole (called a *louvre*) in the roof above. There is not much furniture besides tables and benches. Sir William has a carved chair, and on the wall behind it hangs a curtain embroidered all over by Lady Blanche with a pattern of coloured lozenges and crosses. In a large carved cupboard is kept all the best silver, and the chest is full of linen (napkins, towels, tablecloths, etc.). The floor is covered with rushes. People are not very tidy ; they often throw down bits of meat and bones on the rushes. The dogs like this very much but the rushes smell horribly unless they are often changed. Once everyone used to eat and sleep in the hall all together. But Sir William's grandfather did a good deal of building, so now only the servants sleep in the hall. They must find the benches pretty hard !

If you go back into the screens passage again you will find two doors opposite the hall doors. One goes into the *buttery*, a cool, dark room where wine and ale are kept and some of the food. The other goes into the kitchen where there are always cooks bustling about and good smells of joints roasting before big fires. Beyond the kitchen is a larder where great sides of bacon hang up and much food is stored.

At the end of the screens passage there is a door into a courtyard. If you look now at the plan of the whole house you will see how it goes :

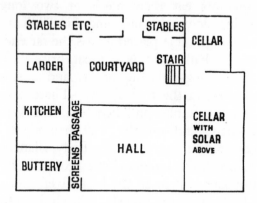

Do you see the staircase in the plan? If we cross the courtyard to this side, we find a doorway into two dark cellars. You can just see the wooden casks of wine standing in rows. Beware of the rats if you go inside! The staircase is close to this doorway. It is an outside stair and goes to the upstairs rooms of the house which are over the cellars. Up here we find a room called the *solar*. It is on the south side of the house and the sun comes streaming through the pointed windows. Now in Latin " Sol " means " sun," and so the solar is really the Sun-Parlour. This is the only room which Sir William and his family have to themselves. Here they all sleep, and often in the daytime you will find Lady Blanche doing her embroidery here while the children are playing draughts or ninepins on the floor. It is the most comfortable room in the house, for it has a real fireplace with a chimney, and there is actually a carpet on the floor ! This is the only carpet in the house and Sir William is very proud of it, for carpets are a novelty in England. He brought it back from a Crusading journey to Palestine.

The walls of the solar are painted with red and white patterns to imitate the hangings which are becoming the fashion. There is quite a lot of furniture as well. In the great wooden bed Sir William and Lady Blanche sleep. The two boys have a bed between them, and Eleanor sleeps in the cradle. Then there is a chest for clothes, a wooden stand called a perch on which to hang clothes, several carved chairs and some stools and benches. I do not think we should find these wooden seats very comfortable, but when Sir William climbs the stair to the solar after a hard, cold day out with his horse and hounds, he finds it very pleasant to sit by the fire. Here he is warming his cold feet :

There is plenty to do in the manor house and no one sits down for long in the solar. To do the work of the manor both inside and out there are many servants, and Sir William and Lady Blanche are kept busy managing them. In the morning Sir William sits in the great hall and does a lot of business. The *steward* brings the manor accounts for him to see, and then tells him all about the troublesome people in the village who have had to be fined in the manor court. Then Sir William discusses the crops with the bailiff, and arranges with him what work the villeins who owe him service shall do. Perhaps they decide how much wool to sell to the wool merchant when he comes, or whether it is time to buy some more cattle. Then perhaps Nicholas Croke, the Reeve, comes in to complain that the bailiff is making the villagers do more work on the lord's land than they ought to. The Reeve, who is chosen by the village, has to oversee all the work the villagers do for their lord.

And sometimes one of the villagers comes up to bring some eggs or a duck for part of his rent. The lord's *falconer* who looks after Sir William's hawks is sure to come in to tell him how the birds are or to show him a new hawk. The bird sits on his wrist securely fastened to it, and over his eyes there is a hood. Sir William looks at his strong, sharp beak, and perhaps he decides to try it out that very day when he goes hawking. Or perhaps the huntsman comes in to tell him where the deer are moving in the deep woods, and if the hounds are ready for the chase. All the time Sir William is talking to these men, people are coming in and out of the hall and there is a fine bustle. Servants rush in and out, village people come in with messages, huntsmen gossip by the fire, and children get in everyone's way.

Sir William has got a bailiff to manage each of his manors and a steward who looks after them all. But still he likes to plan things himself and keep a sharp eye on the account rolls. One of the things he likes to settle himself is whether he will ask the villeins to do the actual work they owe him or whether he will let them pay money instead and then get hired men to do the work. Sometimes he does one and sometimes the other. He says that some of the villeins are so lazy that he would rather have the money! Some of the villeins like to pay the money and have the spare time on their own land. Some would rather do the work. Which way do YOU think is best?

At last Sir William has finished his business! He gets up from the high chair, stretches himself, and shouts for his hawk and horse. Then there is a great clatter outside in the courtyard and in a little while he rides off Here he is hawking:

When he sees a wild duck or *heron* or *crane* he unhoods the hawk and lets it fly from his wrist. Up and up goes the hawk and then down it swoops and strikes with its cruel beak. When the bird falls dead the hawk is trained to return to its master, while a hound fetches in the dead bird. When Sir William is hawking he always wears a strong leather glove on the hand where the hawk perches. Can you see why?

On other days Sir William goes hunting. Here he is in the deep woods hunting the red deer:

Meanwhile Lady Blanche is busy seeing that the cooks do their work in the kitchen. It is a large household and everyone eats a lot, so all day long the cooks are plucking ducks and hens, or chopping the joints for roasting or making great meat pasties. Here are the cooks at work:

Notice the long iron spit for roasting meat in front of the fire. What does the *turnspit* have to do?

Lady Blanche likes to make some special pies and jellies herself. She also makes a lot of medicines to use when anyone in the house or village is ill. Bye and bye, she goes back to the solar and sits beside the fire with her embroidery frame. She is embroidering a picture of people hunting in bright colours. Or perhaps she helps the women servants who weave cloth and make clothes for the household. If it is a sunny day, she goes out to walk in the garden she has made on one side of the house. In summertime she has sweet smelling flowers there—roses, lilies, clove-pinks and *gilly-flowers*. Here she is walking with some visitors :

She grows herbs, too, for cooking and for medicines and there are plenty of vegetables. On the other side of the house there is an orchard with apple, pear, cherry and plum trees. When the fruit is ripening Lady Blanche often goes to see how it is getting on. Sometimes, if she has visitors, she takes them hawking or rabbiting for amusement. Here are the ladies out rabbiting :

The children really have a very good time. **At least,** William and Thomas do. Eleanor is so small she **stays** with her nurse all day. The two boys are supposed **to** have some lessons with the priest, but whenever they **can** they escape and go off to the stables. Anyway, they **have** a lot to learn out of doors. One of the huntsmen is teaching them to ride a horse bareback. He is also teaching them how to manage a hawk, to shoot straight with bow and arrow, to catch hares and rabbits, and many other things. Here is William practising with his bow :

When they get tired they come panting up to the solar stairs and throw themselves down on the carpet by the fire to play a quiet game. Sir William is teaching them how to play chess with a beatifully carved set of chessmen. They have quite a lot of toys as well—hobby horses, balls, skipping ropes, tops and hoops.

There are two big meals in the day for everyone. Dinner is at a strange time : 9 o'clock in the morning ! But then, everyone gets up as soon as it is light so they are ready for a big meal by 9 a.m. Sir William sits in his great chair in the middle of the high-table, and Lady Blanche sits beside him. If there are visitors, they sit beside Sir William and Lady Blanche, and the children are at the end of the table. All the servants sit at the long tables, each in his own place. In front of Sir William there is a big silver saltcellar and a large wooden bowl rimmed with silver called a *mazer* in which the drink is mixed. Except on special occasions the plates are only wooden and the drinking mugs are made of *pewter* which is cheaper than silver. Before the meal begins the family priest says grace and then the servants come in procession from the kitchen carrying great steaming dishes of meat.

There are no spoons and forks. You cut a great piece of meat from the joint with your knife and eat it with your fingers. By the side of each person there is a flat cake of bread called a *trencher*, and you can mop up the gravy with this. For dinner there is usually beef or mutton, with plenty of bread, butter and cheese, and ale to drink. In the time called Lent, when no one must eat any meat, they have herrings and sprats, or fish out of the pond in the park, or sometimes salted fish.

Supper is at 5 in the evening. Usually they eat much the same sort of things as at dinner, but sometimes they have a great feast. Then they fetch out the splendid silver drinking *goblets*, and a big silver bowl which is filled with spiced wine. All round the walls great flaming torches are stuck in iron holders. The fire blazes high and the light dances on the shining silver. Before the meal the chief server blows a call on his trumpet and then the servants march in with basins of water and towels which they present on bended knee to all the feasters on the high-table so that they can wash their hands   Then come all the dishes carried in solemn procession :

This is the menu for one feast :

First Course : Brawn, pottage, veal, mutton, *venison*, hare, rabbit.
Second Course : Pottage, boiled geese, chicken, ducks, pork, pies and pasties.
Third Course : Roasted birds great and small, *capons*, *plovers*, fruits in syrup, pear and apple pie, snapdragon pudding, jellies, pastry ships, cakes.

Whilst everyone eats as much as he can Sir William's *minstrel* plays and sings long stories in poetry called ballads.   And sometimes a travelling acrobat or comic jester turns up and makes everyone roar with laughter as he cuts capers and makes jokes.

Eating and drinking goes on a long time and then everyone is ready to sleep.   The family and the important visitors go upstairs to sleep in the solar, and the servants tumble all over the rushes on the floor, getting as close to the great fire as they can.

WORK TO DO

How long does it take YOU to go to the baker's for a loaf of bread? Five minutes, or more? Have you ever stopped to think how long beforehand people have to plan so as to have the loaves there ready waiting for you? If there were no shops, your family would have to do all the planning and work for itself. That is just what these people in Westwood had to do. It would be no good for them to remember just before dinner that they had run out of bread and send to the shop for it. They had to plan a WHOLE YEAR BEFOREHAND to get their bread, and their meat and clothes too.

So there is always work to do in Westwood. The villagers begin to plan in the autumn when their barns are full of corn. Instead of saying " We have plenty to eat now, we won't bother about next year," they say " Tomorrow is Michaelmas Day and the autumn ploughing begins."

It is still quite dark next morning when : thump! thump! sounds on John's door. " John the Villein," calls a loud voice, " Thou art commanded to plough the lord's land." It is Henry of Combe, the lord's bailiff, going round the village. " Peter Chaffinch! Roger Mouse! Robert Pinchum!" It is cold getting up in the dark, but soon everyone is shouting and stamping as they yoke up the oxen. John Cherryman, the lord's ploughman, is there to tell them what to do. (He sleeps in the shed with the lord's oxen, so you can see bits of straw sticking in his hair.) Bye and bye away go all the villagers to plough the lord's and their own strips in the big East Field.

Here is John the villein ploughing :

Look carefully at the *coulter* which cuts the ground, and behind it the iron *share* and *mouldboard* which slice the earth and turn it over. John keeps his eye fixed straight ahead as he guides the plough, so as to make good straight furrows. At the top of the field he turns round and comes down again, and so he goes on until the whole strip is ploughed.

Notice the wooden yokes or collars of the oxen. How many oxen does John use to drag the plough through the heavy earth? The boy who drives the oxen with the long whip is William. He shouts and sings to the oxen because he says it makes them go better. In wintertime he gets cold and hoarse tramping up and down. Oh, it's cold work ploughing!

Up and down the great field the people are scattered, ploughing different strips. In the midst of work a single bell rings from the church. Everyone stops for a minute and kneels to pray. The people know when the *Sanctus* bell rings that their Rector is holding the daily service in which the whole village worships God. At dinnertime the oxen are unyoked and fed with hay. When they are ploughing his land the lord provides dinner, either a " wet " meal (with ale), or a " dry " one (without). Today it is a wet one and everyone is pleased. They get bread and meat and cheese. Then back again to work they go, until the *Ave* bell rings from the Church, and they kneel again to pray. That is the signal to go home. What will they have to do for the oxen before sitting down to their own suppers ?

Ploughing goes on for many days. If John breaks his plough share against a stone he hurries off to the blacksmith's forge for a new one. He would like to stop and gossip in the warm, but back he must go to speed the plough. There are many other jobs to do as well. Over in the woods Walter Mustard and Simon le Fox are felling trees and carting back timber to the village. People use wood for so many things : buckets, and handles, and ox-yokes—can you go on with the list ? Why do they cut a lot of wood in the autumn ?

Now there is a great noise of grunting and squealing. The swineherd is bringing the pigs back from the woods where they have been getting fat on acorns. Every autumn they have a great pig-killing day. Can you think, why ? Perhaps you would not care to help at the killing but I think you would like the feast of roast pork afterwards ! Great pieces of pork are pickled in tubs like Margaret's, and they hang up sides of bacon to smoke over the fire. Besides this, some of the sheep and cows are killed off too, and they catch and pickle as many fish as possible. You see, they are thinking about food for the long wintertime, and hoping there will be enough to last.

The girls and women are hard at work making thick winter hoods and coats. Then they have to gather great armfuls of brushwood in the woods—some for the lord and some for themselves. And one day they all have to go and get nuts for the lord. If they are not quick, the squirrels are there first, hiding the nuts in their secret winter store.

Wintertime

The ploughed land is stiff and hard now, and the earth must be broken up before the seed is sown. So one cold day John and Margaret go out with great wooden hammers to break the clods on their land. Here they are working. I wonder if Margaret's fingers are numb?

Next comes William with a horse and *harrow*. The harrow has iron teeth underneath to break up the ground into fine soft earth. You can easily guess what Thomas is doing behind with his sling and stones. Which job would you like to do?

At last the big East Field is smooth and soft and ready for sowing with wheat. Everyone sows at the same time, so one day you will see men moving slowly up and down the strips, all sowing. Richard has a *hopper* full of corn, and he takes a handful and, by little and little, casts it into the furrow. It would be no good to put a lot of seed in one place and none in another. Why not? Can you see what the rooks are after and why Richard brings his dog? After sowing, the harrow comes over the ground again to cover the seed with soil. Then it is left to grow. Here is Richard Stout and Gay:

In the darkest and coldest part of the winter, not much can be done out of doors, so folk sit snug at home, mending their tools, or making wooden plates, or baskets, or boots. It is difficult to see, and rushlights get few and precious. Everyone looks anxiously at the stores. They ask: " Will the wood last out to give us good fires ? How much pork is left in the tub ? Is there enough hay for the cattle ?" In the sheds the poor sows and oxen begin to grow thin, for the hay is very short. It's a hard time in the village while the cold lasts !

Spring Comes

The winter rains stop at last, the sun is warmer at mid-day and the ground begins to dry up. Now there is more work to do in the fields. The second great field— the West Field—is ploughed and harrowed and sown with oats and barley. John sings this little song as he works :

> Oats and beans and barley grow,
> Oats and beans and barley grow ;
> Do you or I or anyone know
> How oats and beans and barley grow ?

Do you know a tune to that song?

Now the time of the singing of birds begins, and green buds shoot on the trees. Now the plum and apple trees must be pruned to get good fruit in the summer. You must take a sharp knife and cut off shoots cunningly, so that the tree does not grow too quickly, but makes fruit-buds instead. Here they are pruning the lord's orchard. Simon le Fox is thinking to himself: "Why should Sir William have all these apples to himself when WE do the work?" So before he goes he has a good look at the orchard wall. You will hear more about this later.

Now the fresh young grass is springing everywhere, and the sheep and cattle are turned out to graze. Some of the cows are so thin that they can hardly totter out, but the grass is juicy and young, and soon they will be getting fat. Every morning the cowherd goes down the street blowing his horn, and the cows come trotting out of each gate. All day he guards them on the common and at night brings them in again. One of the cows is shrewd and wicked with her horn, but the cowherd knows how to manage her! I don't know how you would like to meet the village bull. He is actually allowed to run loose with the cows. This is all right when he is good-tempered, but one hot day when he was irritated by flies he chased Roger Mouse across the common and up into a tall tree, where the poor man sat in a great state of fright until the bull had been shut up.

Here you see a shepherd grazing his flock on the common :

The shepherds lead their sheep to the fresh young grass, and while they watch they make whistle pipes from reeds and play tunes on them. Each shepherd trains his dog to go after the sheep by calling " Go seek, seek, seek." To call him back, he cries " Come home, home, home." The shepherds have to watch by night, too, in the spring-time, for the ewes and lambs must be cared for.

All the animals are glad to get out again. In the woods the pigs are grunting joyfully as they nose among the dead leaves or crunch the roots that the swineherds dig up for them. Now summer is coming in and everyone is glad. Birds are nesting, lambs are playing, and in the great fields the green corn is springing. One day a monk who loved all these things wrote this song :

Summer is i-cumen in,
Loudly sing cuckoo !
Groweth seed and bloweth *mead*,
And springeth the wood new.

Ewe bleateth after lamb,
Cow *loweth* after calf,
Bullock rouses and *buck* browses,
Merrily sing cuckoo !

Cuckoo, cuckoo, well sing thee, cuckoo :
Nor cease thee never now ;
Sing cuckoo now, sing cuckoo,
Sing cuckoo, sing cuckoo now !

Do you know the tune the monk made for those words ? Perhaps it was one he heard the shepherds singing.

All this time the third great field has been lying fallow. But giving it a rest is not enough to make it grow a good crop again. Do you know why you manure your garden ? The villagers would tell you that you must put back some goodness into the ground to make up for what you took out in the last crop. So they put up hurdles and fold the sheep on this field in order to manure the ground well. They also dig up and bring cart loads of some good earth called *marl* (which is a mixture of clay and lime) and spread it all over the field. After this they dig ditches to drain the water off and plough up the fallow field.

Summertime

At Midsummer the days are long and the villagers are out in the fields from dawn till dusk. Down by the stream the tall rich grass in the hay-meadow is fenced round, while each man's share is marked off with stakes. If the cows and sheep break into the meadow now, they would spoil all the hay for next winter. John caught his son Thomas catching butterflies in the hay-meadow one day and gave him such a hiding for trampling down the grass. But some parents do not look after their children so well. Agnes Redhead let her little girl Joan run right across it one day, but Nicholas Croke the Reeve saw her, and reported it to the next manor court, and Agnes had to pay 6d.

The young corn has to be fenced as well to keep out wandering sheep and cows. Yet still the wicked animals seem to get in ! The Rector had to pay a fine of 4d the other day because his cow got in the corn.

A special man called the Hayward guards the hay and corn. Early and late he must range round and spy on the fields. He has a horn to blow when he chases animals out of the crops. When he finds stray beasts he puts them in the *pound* which is a square pen in the middle of the village. Then the owner has to pay a fine to get them out again. The villagers have a rule that the Hayward must always have the strips of corn on the edge of the field. You can think out for yourself why they do this.

Robert Pinchum the Hayward is a lazy fellow ! One hot afternoon when he ought to have been spying after the animals, he lay under a hedge sleepily watching the big white clouds sail by. Suddenly there was a rustle and he opened his eyes just in time to see a strange man slinking into the wood with something big under his arm. Robert pretended he had not seen him and shut his eyes again. This was very bad, for by the village rules he ought to have jumped up crying " Thief !" and run after him. Then all the people would stop whatever they were doing and join in the chase. This is called raising the hue and cry.

Luckily someone else had seen the thief and in a few minutes Robert heard the men go running by crying " Thief ! Thief ! " But still he did not move. It was far too hot to run ! Then he fell sound asleep, and the next thing he knew was the Reeve shaking him and crying " Wake up, lazy good-for-nothing ! The sheep are in the meadow and the cows are in the corn !"

He ran fast enough now, but a lot of damage was done before he got them out again. At last the men came back from the chase, but the thief had got away, and there was old Mother Slopper wailing that her grey goose was gone. Then the Reeve turned round to Robert and said : " Where were YOU when the hue and cry was raised ?" Robert was fairly caught and at the next manor court he had to pay a double fine for not raising the hue and cry, and for letting the animals get among the crops. If you ask him whether he has had a nice nap today he gets quite angry !

The grass in the hay-meadow is high enough to hide in now, with moon daisies shining in it and dragon flies skimming over. Now when the sun shines everyone goes down to mow the hay. They use long curved *scythes* like this :

The scythe swings through the stems with a gentle swishing sound, and the cut grass falls softly in heaps. It looks easy to do, but you have to be careful not to cut your own feet with the scythe ! In a day or two they toss the hay with pitch-forks. Why do they do this ? It's real sport for the children who throw hay all over each other and play battles with it. The sun dries the hay. If it is cold or wet everyone gets worried because the hay will be spoilt. " Make hay while the sun shines," is what they say. When it is made the hay is stacked in hayricks.

The villagers have to make the lord's hay as well. They often grumble a lot about this, but for doing it they each get three quarters of wheat, one ram, one pat of butter and a piece of the lord's best cheese. And they play a sort of game too. Each man is allowed to carry away from the lord's hay as much as he can lift on his scythe. But if the handle breaks and the bundle drops, then he loses it. Everyone crowds round to see the game. Roger Mouse is so timid that he carries away a tiny bit and everyone laughs. John is careful and gets a nice tidy pile, but the biggest laugh is against greedy Adam Doget who picks up almost more than he can lift, gets halfway up the field with it, and then crack! goes the handle, and he loses the lot.

There are hundreds of jobs to do now in the village, and if you walk round you will find everyone busy. Make a list for yourself of all the jobs to be done in summer time. William Cherryman is mending the roof of his house. Walter Mustard is helping Bray the Miller mend the sails of his windmill. The blacksmith is sharpening scythes and sickles for reaping on his *grindstone*. Joan and Agnes, the lord's dairymaids, have been milking the ewes. They have cows and goats to milk as well, in the early morning and afternoon. Then they have all the cheese and butter to make.

The Reeve is going round the village keeping his eye on everything. He must never be slothful or sleepy, for he must see that everyone is doing the right work, and that nothing is wasted, or stolen.

The next picture tells its own story. How would you like to help the bee-keeper?

Bees are very important to the villagers, because they have no sugar and use honey for sweetening. Why have they no sugar? The bee-keeper makes round hives for the bees out of twigs, and sets them in a warm place. Then he has to watch out to catch the bees when they all fly away in a swarm round the Queen Bees. If you know someone who keeps bees, ask him how he deals with a swarm. May is the best month for swarming, when sweet flowers blossom everywhere with honey for the bees in their throats. All day long in May, June and July the bees gather honey and store it in the hive. The bee-keeper knows a rhyme about bees :

A swarm of bees in May is worth a load of hay,
A swarm of bees in June is worth a silver spoon,
A swarm of bees in July isn't worth a fly.

47

Why do you think a July swarm is no good ? When the bees have built their golden honeycombs, the bee-keeper takes out the honey, carefully leaving enough for the bees for the winter. He has to give so much honey to the lord, and the rest goes to the villagers. Bees are very valuable, and one night Widow Ducie had her best hive stolen. She complained in the manor court, but everyone said it must have been a stranger. How could he take a whole hive of bees without getting stung? they said. A month later when Peter Mead was rabbiting on the common, he found the hive tucked snugly away in a secret place among the gorse bushes. It was just in time for Widow Ducie to get a nice lot of honey, but no one ever discovered who the thief was.

One day in July there is a great sheep-washing. How the sheep hate it ! You can hear them baa-ing a mile off as they are driven into a pen by the river. Several men wade into the water, and then someone catches a sheep and pushes it, kicking and struggling, into the stream. When they have washed it, they push it out into another pen. After sheep-washing comes *sheep-shearing*. You can think for yourself why they do things in this order. Each man catches a sheep, holds him down between his legs and cuts the thick wool off the sheep's back with a big pair of shears. If he does this carefully, all the wool comes off in one big piece, called a *fleece*. If the sheep wriggles suddenly and the shears cut it, the man dabs on tar to stop it bleeding, but a good sheep-shearer does not often hurt the animals. When he has finished, the sheep trots off looking rather thin and forlorn, but in the hot weather he must be glad to have lost his winter coat.

The villagers have to wash the lord's sheep as well.

One day when the lord's bailiff came round to order everyone to go next day for the sheep-washing, there was much grumbling because people said the lord's sheep ought to have been washed with the rest, and they wanted to get the corn cut while the fine weather lasted. Now, Simon le Fox was a mischief-maker. He went round that night to people's houses saying, " Why SHOULD we wash the lord's sheep ?" So next morning all but seven went off to cut their corn. Those seven had a hard day, but they got a good meal from the lord of meat, and bread and pottage and ale, and at the next meeting of the manor court the rest were sorry they had listened to Simon le Fox. For the bailiff asked the court : " What is the custom of the manor ?" And the villagers had to answer truly : " The custom is that we wash the lord's sheep on the day he commands." Then the bailiff fined all the village, except the seven, 6 shillings and 8 pence for not coming to wash the lord's sheep.

By the end of July, everyone is busy reaping the yellow corn.

Notice the difference between the curved sickles used for corn-cutting and the scythes used for hay-cutting. The man behind is Nicholas Croke, the Reeve. Can you guess what he does with his stick if one man gets behind? As the corn is cut, it is tied into sheaves by hand. Do we cut corn like this today?

Here they are stacking the sheaves together in the field:

And now here they are carrying the harvest home to the barns:

The wheels have spikes on them to stick into the ground. I don't think the road goes uphill quite so steeply as the man has drawn it, but you can see that they are having a job with it.

Soon the lord's corn is stowed in his great dark barn, and each villager stacks his own in a rick or barn. But first of all everyone gives part of his crop to the Rector who stores it in the *tithe-barn*. This is really a gift to God in thanks for the harvest. Harvesting is the most important and anxious time of the year, for if the harvest is good there will be enough bread for next year. But if the harvest is poor or gets spoilt by rain, the village will go very hungry, or even starve in the winter. So people look anxiously at the weather, and when the last of the corn is safely gathered home, they have a grand feast of rejoicing, the Harvest Home.

Now all the fruit trees in the village hang down low with the weight of their fruit. There are apples and pears and plums, and out on the common boys and girls pick blackberries and sloes and nuts. Gilbert the swineherd is knocking down acorns from the oak trees for his pigs. How they scramble and squeal for them !

Here is a little song which someone made about the harvest and all the nice things which men and animals enjoy then :

In time of harvest merry it is enow,
Pears and apples hang thick on the bough,
The Hayward bloweth merry his horn,
In every field ripe is the corn,
The grapes hang on the vine,
Sweet is true love and fine.

Look at this picture !

I think you can tell the story of what is happening for yourself, but this is how the story was told afterwards in the manor court :

Sir steward, the bailiff makes complaint of Simon le Fox who sent his son Thomas over the lord's wall and commanded him to carry off every manner of fruit. And when the bailiff heard the fruit being knocked down he marvelled who this could be and at once entered the lord's orchard and found the boy right high on a *custard apple* tree, which he had cultivated for the lord's use because of its goodness. He made him come down and asked him by whose sending he entered the lord's orchard over walls well closed on all sides, and the boy answered that Simon his father bade him enter it and urged him on to the trees with the best fruit. So the bailiff let the boy carry off all that he had.

Simon had to pay a fine of 6 shillings and he vowed that was too dear for a basket of apples!

Autumn Again

The cut corn is not yet ready to make into bread. First, the grains of corn have to be *threshed* (or beaten) out of their husks. So now you may hear thump! thump! coming from the barn, and looking in you will see two men threshing the sheaves of corn with jointed sticks called flails.

Meanwhile, the women shovel up the grain and the empty shells (called *chaff*) and throw them into the air. The heavy grain falls straight down, but the chaff is blown into a separate heap. This is called *winnowing*. They pour the grain into sacks, but keep the straw and chaff for the sheep and cattle.

Now at last John is ready to take a sack of corn to the windmill on top of the hill to be ground into flour.

The wind turns the sails and the sails turn the two great grind stones in the mill. Between them the corn is ground into flour. Before John takes his sack of flour away he has to give Bray the miller some of it in return for grinding it and the lord has to have some too because he owns the mill.

When John brings the flour home, Margaret can make her bread at last ! She mixes the flour with water and makes flat loaves which she takes to the lord's big oven to bake. The lord insists that everyone should bake in his oven, and of course she has to pay a loaf to do this.

You see that it takes a long time and much work to get flour for bread. While the villagers are still threshing and grinding THIS year's corn, they are already starting to plough up the field for NEXT year's corn. For they are always thinking ahead.

FUN AND GAMES

Are you wondering whether the people of Westwood ever have a holiday ? If you asked him, John would probably answer : " Oh, there are plenty of feast days, and Sundays too."

Early on Sunday morning all the folk are dressed in their brightest clothes, for the church bell calls them. First comes the service called Mattins and then the service of the Mass. The Rector says Mass on weekdays as well but if the people are too busy in the fields, then they always go on Sunday.

The villagers are very proud of the new church which they helped to build themselves. Inside, in the first part (the *nave*), all the people kneel or stand for the service. Only the old folk have seats. There is a step up to the second part (the *chancel*), where the priest stands. The altar at the end is covered with beautiful embroidery in green and blue and gold, and by it stand tall shining candlesticks. There are pictures on the walls and in the windows, painted in bright colours of blue and scarlet and gold. These tell stories from the Bible and the lives of the saints. Everything is bright and gay with colour, and as the people look round they remember that everything inside the church has been given as a present by someone.

Just below the altar there is a marble figure of a knight lying in a little hollow in the wall. This is in memory of Sir William's father. It stood in the old church and has been carefully moved into the new one and decorated with gold and vermilion. If Sir William is at home, he will be kneeling with the people at service, he and all his family.

At Mass the Rector blesses the Holy Water, and afterwards one of the villagers, called the Parish Clerk, carries it round and sprinkles every house, so that all the families may live in peace and happiness during the next week.

Some people go again to church for Evensong but for the rest of Sunday the people mostly enjoy themselves with games and music.

Nearly everyone makes his own bow and arrows and practises hard, for it is a great thing to be a good archer. To make the bow they choose elm-wood or yew, because these woods are tough and yet bend well. The bow-string is made of hemp. For arrows they use oak, birch or ash, and each arrow must have a forked head one end and grey goose feathers the other. If you want to be very gay, like Robin Hood, you put peacock's feathers on your arrows. It takes a strong man to bend a full-sized longbow and string it ready to shoot. Here you see some of them practising archery at the butts with long-bows :

Then they play a game with sticks which looks like hockey, and of course they go in for wrestling. What is the difference between wrestling and boxing? Sometimes two men climb on the shoulders of two others and wrestle pickaback.

Some of their games, for instance skittles and bowls, we still like playing. Here are the villagers playing bowls:

People are fond of playing games with a board marked out in squares. Like us, they play chess and draughts and backgammon. Can you play any of these games? The children have a board-game called Nine Men's Morris. Two can play it: you have nine " men " each and put them down in turn on the squares of the board. The game is to stop the other one getting three in a row. Try it yourself; you can draw squares for the board and use buttons or anything you like for the men.

For another game, called Fox and Geese, you have seventeen pieces called geese, and one black one for the fox. You put these on the board with the fox in the middle, and the game is to shut up the other person's fox so that he cannot move. You move your geese one square at a time, but if you let one goose get on a square with a space behind it, then the fox can take it.

Here are two people playing on a board. What do you think the game is?

I wonder how many of the games the boys and girls play are like yours? One is called Titter-totter which is the same as our see-saw. Barley-break is a kind of "tag" played among the corn sheaves, with one sheaf for "home" and one for "prison" for those who get caught. They call the game in the next picture Hoodman Blind. What do you call it?

One of their blindfold games is called **Hot Cockles**. One boy kneels down blindfolded; he puts one hand, open, on his own back and cries " Hot Cockles, Hot !" Another boy hits his open hand, and he must guess who has hit him.

Have you ever played singing games like Here we go Round the Mulberry Bush, or Green Gravel ? The children in Westwood sing songs very like these. One of their singing games is called **Frog in the Middle**.

One player sits down with his legs tucked underneath, and the rest stand round in a ring, pushing and pulling him while he tries to catch them without getting up. This is the song they sing while they play :

Hey, hey, hi, hey, hey, hi !
Frog in the middle and there shall lie,
He can't get out and he can't get in,
Hey, hey, hi, hey, hey, hi !

In the next picture you will see games that you know very well.

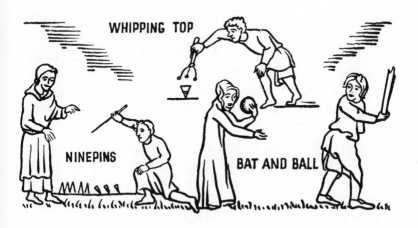

WHIPPING TOP

NINEPINS

BAT AND BALL

There are no bank holidays in Westwood. You can think out for yourself why not. But there are plenty of feast days or festivals. These are the holy days of the Church when everyone has a holiday. We will begin with one of the most joyful—Christmas. Everyone has twelve days' holiday. On Christmas Eve the Yule logs, which Sir William gives to everyone, are dragged home from the woods. Then they light great festival fires and decorate the houses with holly, ivy, yew and mistletoe.

Just before midnight on Christmas Eve everyone

goes up through the black starry night to the Midnight Mass at the church. There is a model of the stable at Bethlehem with the manger and the cattle and figures of Joseph, Mary, the Shepherds and the Christ Child. Everyone gathers round, singing carols, and dancing, and rocking the cradle. In the morning the new bells ring their gayest peal calling people to church again. Some of the village folk act a play of the Christ Child in the church, and everyone watches intently as the angels appear, singing " Glory to God in the Highest," and the shepherds find their way to Bethlehem to worship the newborn king.

After that there is feasting and festival for everyone. Sir William gives a feast for all his tenants in the great hall of the manor house. Each man takes with him his own plate and mug and napkin. The great fire is roaring in the middle of the hall, and torches or candles are stuck on spikes round the walls. The chief server blows a horn and everyone sits down at the long tables, which are laid with flat cakes of bread for plates, great salt cellars and big wooden bowls of ale. The lord and his family greet them all and sit down at the high-table. Now the bagpipes strike up, and a procession comes from the kitchen. First comes William the shepherd, playing his bagpipes, and then the servers, two by two, carrying hot steaming dishes full of good things. There is hare and rabbit, roast goose and chicken, beef and pork and other roast meats ; afterwards come jellies, fruit in syrup and cakes. Everyone eats a lot and gets merry. At the end of the feast, the tables are cleared away for games and dancing. Two men have a mock fight with swords. Then they all play Hoodman Blind. Now there are some minstrels coming in with their instruments:

The last has a harp, the next a vielle (fiddle), the next a pipe and tabor (drum), and the first two trumpets. Do these instruments look like ones we play today? Everyone listens as they sing ballads about bold men and brave deeds.

Then all the merrymakers begin to dance to the sound of pipe and tabor. Sometimes they do a carol in a circle, singing as they dance, and sometimes they dance in a line. Here is one kind of dance:

And here is another dance :

Now there is a noise of shouting and laughing out-side and a rap at the door.   In come the village *mummers*. Here are some of them :

The people pretend they do not know that all these strange creatures with animal heads are just their village friends. Some have deer horns, and there are monkeys, goats, rabbits and asses. They do a sword-dance with short sticks for swords, and then one sweeps a large circle in the middle of the hall, and calls in the players one by one. On page 85 you will find a piece of a play rather like the one they act about St. George and the Turkish Knight.

Fun goes on all through the twelve days of Christmas. The mummers go round from house to house, acting their plays, dancing and singing carols. At every house they get cakes or else ale in a big wooden bowl, called the wassail bowl. On Twelfth Night (January 5th) there is another feast and then the decorations come down. Christmas is ended !

The Monday after Twelfth Night is called Plough Monday. All the ploughmen in the village black their faces and yoke themselves, instead of the oxen, to their ploughs. They go round the village with seven dancers jumping and singing round them, and they act another play in which a man on a hobby horse fights the Wild Worm and the dragon. The beginning of the play goes something like this :

> We are come over the mire and the moss,
> We dance an Hobby Horse ;
> A dragon you shall see,
> And a wild worm for to flee.
> Still we are all brave jovial boys,
> And take delight in Christmas toys.
> Come in, come in, thou Hobby Horse,
> Come in, come in, thou bonny wild worm,
> Come in, come in, thou dragon stout.

Then they begin to fight. At the end of the play they collect money for a candle in church, called the Plough Light, and for a feast for all the ploughmen.

At Candlemas (February 2nd) there is a procession with lights, and all their candles are blessed. After that comes Shrove Tuesday when everyone eats pancakes and plays football through the middle of the village. On the next day, Ash Wednesday, all the villagers go to church, where ashes are sprinkled over them to show that they are sorry for all the wrong things they have done. Then begins Lent, a solemn time with few feasts, when all the gay colours and figures in the church are covered with grey veils, and a grey veil hangs in front of the alter to hide it.

On Palm Sunday the people remember how children waved palm branches in front of Christ as He rode into Jerusalem, so they decorate the church with green branches and everyone is given a bit to keep. Then comes Good Friday—dark and solemn because Christ died on that day.

But soon Easter Day dawns, when Christ rose from the dead, and on that morning the whole village gets up early to see the sun rise. It is springtime now—the time for feasts and merriment—and the village has fourteen days' holiday. All the grey veils are gone from the church, which is full of yellow spring flowers—primroses, daffodils, and so on. The village well is decorated with green boughs and blessed by the priest. The mummers come round again with shouts of laughter to act their play of St. George and the Turkish Knight, and the children all get Easter eggs—not chocolate ones, but real eggs which have been painted red and yellow and decorated with patterns.

There are different feasts and festivals all through the

summer. When all the ploughing is done the lord gives a feast to his tenants; they bring their wives, and have a whole ox to roast, besides 200 herrings, cheeses, and two bushels of peas, with salt and garlic to taste, and ale to drink. The first of May—May Day—is a time for frolics. On the evening before, all the young folk go to the woods for branches of white flowering hawthorn and green boughs. Then they decorate all the houses, especially the doors, and sing this song:

> All in this pleasant evening, together come are we,
> For the summer springs so fresh, green and gay;
> We'll tell you of a blossom and buds on every tree,
> Drawing near to the merry month of May.

On May Day itself everyone in the village wears green, with posies of flowers, and all the young folk go a-maying. First they come dancing round the village, in and out of all the houses, with a pipe and tabor for music. They are dressed in all sorts of strange ways. One man is covered with green bushes, and they call him Jack i' the Green. One man rides a hobby horse. One has a fox's head and tail on. Six or eight have bells on their ankles and carry short sticks to do a Morris Dance. Two are chosen to be the Lord and Lady of the May, with garlands of flowers for crowns. As they dance, they sing May songs. Then they all gather in the middle of the village round a young green tree which is the Maypole. They hang a big garland on it and there they dance and sing and feast all day.

Next comes Rogation-tide, which means " asking-time." The villagers all go in procession from the church with the priest in front, all round the fields and boundaries of the village. The children carry long sticks and green boughs, and some people have banners with bells on them. At certain trees they stop while the priest reads from the Bible and blesses all the springing crops, asking God to give them a good harvest. Then they sing a psalm praising God for all the trees and growing plants. Do we ever have a Rogation-tide procession today?

At Whitsuntide there are more plays, made up and acted by the village folk, and on Midsummer Night they light a great bonfire and have a feast round it. They have wrestling matches, with a whole ram for the prize, and they try to climb a greasy pole to get a leg of mutton on the top. Finally, they take a wooden wheel to the top of the hill, set fire to it, and send it rolling down the hill with bright sparks flying.

There are many other festivals and saints days in the year, and on nearly all of them villagers have a holiday and do something special. On Corpus Christi Day there is another procession and a play. On Michaelmas Day they have a big feast. Later on, when the days are growing dark, comes All Hallow E'en (October 31st), when the children have fruit and nuts to eat and play at bobbing apples. This is a game in which you try to get apples out of a tub of water with your teeth alone. People frighten each other with stories of ghosts on this night. Next day, the festival of All Saints, fires are lighted on the hills and the children run round from house to house singing :

Soul, soul, for a soul-cake,
Pray, good mistress, for a soul-cake.

68

And the women always give them little cakes specially baked for this day. Next day is All Souls' Day, when the church bell rings for the souls of the villagers who have died. Then the children eat their little soul-cakes.

Soon after that the children begin thinking about Christmas again. So the year goes round with feasts and merrymaking. Have you noticed that nearly all the village holidays are the church holy days ? That is what our word " holiday " means—holy-day. The priest tells people to stop work and be merry on these special days, and so they make their jollifications. Do you like the ways in which they amuse themselves ? Would YOU enjoy doing these things ? We have very different sorts of amusement today, but most people still keep the great festivals, especially Christmas. I wonder if you do any of the same things at Christmas time that the people of Westwood did ? Which of the other festivals do we still keep ?

LAWBREAKERS IN THE VILLAGE

You may want to know whether people ever get up to any tricks in Westwood. Well, we have already heard one or two bad stories about some of the villagers. When a lot of people live together like this, you can't expect them all to behave properly ALL the time. The only thing you can do is to make some good rules or laws about the things they must not do, and then try to punish those that break the laws.

People with quarrelsome tongues are a great nuisance. Such people have to be fined in the manor court. Sometimes people have to be punished for silly tricks. One day some of the boys caught all the pigs in the woods and tied their feet together so that they could not move. They hid them away in the thick bushes so that it took the swineheard a long time to find them. Very often indeed there are thefts and house-breakings to punish. Some people are born scoundrels! They pull wool off other people's sheep, they take pieces of clothing hung out to dry, they remove hens by night and pocket eggs. But the villagers soon get to know who the scoundrels are and keep a strict eye on them!

Some of the rules are made by the whole village for the good of everyone. Some are made by the lord for his special benefit. He has a rule that no one can take fish out of his pond or hunt deer in his woods. I don't know whether you think that is fair, but I will tell you what happened one day. Walter of the Moor's wife was ill and had lain in bed a whole month. She would eat little but kept asking Walter to get her a fine perch, which is a fish. Now the only place for this fish was the lord's pond, so one moonlit night poor Walter went out stealthily into the lord's park and came to the pond. And there he saw the fish playing in the water and longed to take just one for his wife. So he lay down on the bank and slid his arm softly into the water and without splash or sound took one perch and carried it home to his wife. Now I wonder if YOU would have punished him in the court?

The lord has a keeper named John, who guards the deer in the woods. One day when he went to look for a stray hawk he saw Geoffrey of the Moor and his huntsman come into the woods with two greyhounds and go up hill and down dale spying what they would shoot. Away went Keeper John helter-skelter to the village and fetched up two men to come back with him to see what Geoffrey would do. As soon as they were inside the woods they saw him in full chase with his hounds after a fine buck. He took an arrow, barbed broad and long, and shot the buck right through the flank, and skinned it, and covered it with bushes. Then he crept quietly out of the wood. He did not know that he had been watched, but when he came out Keeper John met him and said : " Fair friend Geoffrey, seemingly thou hast done right great folly, and peradventure thou hast done it more than once." Now Geoffrey was very angry, but he did not answer and strode away. Keeper John went back into the wood, found the buck, and then looked for the arrow and found it. Next time the court met he had the arrow there and the two men as witnesses to what they had seen. So Geoffrey could deny nothing, and was fined £10.

Whenever there is a dispute or someone breaks a rule, the matter is brought to the manor court. This is an important meeting of all the villagers which is held every three weeks in the hall of the manor house. Anyone who has a quarrel or complaint, anyone who has lost or found something, or has something to say, brings it up in the court where it is discussed and settled. Twice a year, at Easter and at Michaelmas, the lord's chief servant, the steward, holds a larger court when many people who have done wrong are punished.

First of all, however, the villagers have to catch the wrongdoer, and this is sometimes very difficult to do. There is only one policeman in the village, and there is no proper prison in which wrongdoers can be locked up. So the villagers have special ways of catching and keeping thieves and other law-breakers. When a boy is twelve years old, he has to join a little group of men called a *tithing*, under a leader called the head *tithingman*. Everyone in the village belongs to a tithing, and if any one of the group does anything wrong, the others in the tithing have to catch him and bring him to the court. If they let him go and are found out, they get punished. Do you think that is a good way of catching criminals ? Why do we not need such a plan today ?

If someone is caught stealing and starts to run away, all the people have to stop what they are doing and go after him as fast as they can, shouting and blowing horns and making as much noise as they can. All the dogs come barking behind, and there is such a hullabaloo that the people in the next village often hear the noise and if the thief comes their way they join in the chase as well. The village has raised the hue and cry ! Quite often the thief escapes into the forest where he can hide. If he once gets to a church he is safe inside, for no one is allowed to go and drag him out. Sometimes people wait outside and try to starve him out, but often he is able to slip out on a dark night and so escape. Of course they catch some thieves, and all these, together with all the people who have done bad work or broken the rules of the village, are brought before the manor court.

THE MANOR COURT

We will pay a visit to a manor court which is being held one Wednesday morning just after Michaelmas. Some days before, the lord's bailiff goes round the village summoning everyone to attend the court. If they don't come they may get fined. Then the lord's steward (who is more important than the bailiff) arrives from one of the lord's other manors to be the chairman of the court. The clerk comes with him to write down all that is decided. This is most important because sometimes people forget what they did decide. Then they can look back to see what the clerk has written. He sits at a table in the manor-hall, and writes on a long piece of *parchment* —sometimes two or three feet long and nine or twelve inches wide. Measure out how big this is. On this long strip the clerk writes down all the names of people who have to be tried and all sorts of other things. When he is not using it he rolls it up, and so it is called a Court Roll.

In the hall the bailiff has put some benches on which the head tithingmen and other important people sit. The rest stand, but everyone in the village helps to decide who has done wrong and who has not. When they have done this, the steward decides how the wrong-doers shall be punished. Then he gives orders to the bailiff to see that the punishment is carried out.

Early in the morning men and women start coming into the hall, gossiping about the business of the day. Some of them look very gloomy. Can you guess why?

About 9 o'clock the steward and the clerk walk in. This is what they look like:

The clerk has three or four heavy rolls to bring. These are the rolls of the last court, in case anyone wants to look back and see what happened. He sits at the table and gets out his *quill pen* which is a feather pointed at one end. Then he unrolls the parchment on which he is going to write. Already he has written the title of the court in large letters:

> The court of the manor of Westwood, held on Wednesday, the Feast of St. Matthew, in the third year of the reign of King Edward I.

He has to be very quick in writing down the cases while the court is going on, and so he shortens his words when-

ever possible. He writes everything in Latin   This is
what the court roll looks like :

The steward wants to start, so he calls a man named
the *beadle* who stands up and calls for silence, crying
" Oyez, oyez, oyez ! " which means " Listen, listen,
listen !" The first business is to name twelve older men,
usually the head tithingmen, who take a solemn oath that
they will bring forward everyone who has done wrong,
and report any trouble which has happened since the
last court. The steward stands up, and, with the beadle
by his side holding a book, he says " Hold up your hands.
You are to find out and present all who have done wrong.
You are to report all those who are absent. You are to
tell us if there are any twelve years old and more who are
not in a tithing   You are to say if order has been kept

in the village, and if there are any thieves or poachers. You must tell us if any bridges have been broken or paths altered or streams spoilt. And you must tell us of any who have brewed ale or baked their bread badly, or sold it unfairly."

The headmen then go out and discuss together all the things they will have to say. If they forget anything and the steward finds out, they will be fined. While the court is waiting for them, the steward hears excuses sent by those who have not been able to come. If a man is ill or away on the king's service, he is excused. But not every excuse is allowed. Richard the Smith brings an excuse from his neighbour Robert at the Stream that he is ill in bed. But that very morning the bailiff had seen Robert feeding his pigs at the back of the house! So Robert is ordered to appear at the next court when he will be fined, and Richard is fined threepence now.

At last the tithingmen come back. First, they read out the names of the people in the tithings. They declare that two boys, William and Roger, are now twelve years old but have not yet been enrolled in a tithing; each is fined threepence. They say that William the Carpenter who is the head of one of the tithings has not come to court and has sent no excuse. He is therefore fined sixpence. At that moment a man runs into court with a message that William has been kicked by a horse that morning. So the fine is excused. The clerk sighs as he rapidly crosses out the fine in the roll.

Then the tithingmen begin to accuse those who have done wrong. They say that Richard Pye on a Monday night before Michaelmas broke into John Lovel's house by making a hole in the plaster wall, and that he stole brass pots and pans and a piece of cloth, all worth ten shillings. Richard is not present, so the bailiff is ordered to see that he comes to the next court, and to take two of his oxen to make sure that he attends.

Then the tithingmen say that Bray the Miller has dug deep holes in the road to get clay, and that the road is dangerous at night now. The bailiff is told to enquire into this, and Bray will probably be fined next time.

Hugo at the Hall is accused of stopping up a small stream which runs down the village street. The headmen say he has been cleaning out some stables and has left a great heap of filth by the roadside. Not only has it stopped up the stream, but it is a nuisance to others because it smells so foul. Hugo is fined twelve pence.

The chief tithingmen say that on a Monday after the feast of St. Luke, the Hayward's wife and a neighbour were baking at the lord's oven. They began to quarrel because one had lost a loaf, and they fought each other with their fists and tore at each other's hair. Their husbands came up and also joined in the fight. The men are fined and their wives severely warned.

Do you remember about Agnes the gossip and how she quarrelled with Alice ? In the last court the tithingmen complained that Agnes was a bad gossip because she said untrue things about people. She had said that she was NOT a bad gossip, so she had been told to bring five people to the next court who would say that she was telling the truth. She is now in court with her five friends; but they all say different things and everyone agrees that Agnes is a malicious (or bad) gossip. So they decide to punish her by putting her into the ducking stool next Sunday. This is what the ducking stool looks like :

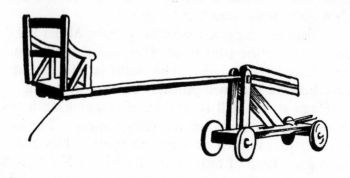

She will be tied in, and then ducked three times in the village pond at the end of the street. She is a bad-tempered old woman and the bailiff has to push her out of the court while she shouts angrily.

Then the tithingmen tell Peter Chaffinch's story of how he was robbed by night, and they accuse Adam Doget. But Adam comes and says that he slept all night at Simon le Fox's house, and Simon swears that this is true. Many people think that these two have plotted together to do the robbery, but there are no witnesses and the stolen goods cannot be found. So no case can be proved against Adam and he gets off.

The tithingmen then declare that all three butchers in the village, Alexander Longshanks, James Gotobed and Mathew Peabody, have been selling bad meat. Each is fined sixpence, and James, who has done it before, is to be put in the stocks. The stocks look like this :

Thomas Fisher has been keeping his fish too long, and people complain that he has sold it to them stinking and rotten, so that they have been taken sick. He declares that the fish was good, and is told to bring six people to the next court to swear that he is speaking the truth.

The tithingmen also tell a sad tale about Mark Everard, one of the lord's servants. In the last court he was ordered to seize three young cows belonging to Robert Pinchum, and keep them in the pound, because Robert had not yet paid a fine he owed. As Mark was driving in the cattle, Robert and his two sons knocked him down with a staff and nearly broke his head. They then drove away their cows. Mark now comes with his head tied up, and tells his tale, and produces two witnesses who saw it all. Robert is fined two shillings for damaging one of the lord's servants.

Next, villagers have to be chosen to do various jobs for the coming year. First, the village constable (or police-man) is chosen. His job is to keep order. He will have to see that Agnes is ducked next Sunday! The man chosen does not like the job, so he tries to refuse, but the steward tells him sharply that he must do it. Would YOU like to be constable ?

Then two men are chosen to be aletasters. They have to go round the village to see that everyone is brewing ale in the right way and selling it at the right price. In the court the aletasters for last year have a list of those who have broken the rules, six in all; each is find threepence, and Meg Merry, who is one of them, grumbles loudly because last time she was let off. The beadle tells her to be silent.

All the people who have bought land have to come now and declare it. Each one pays a small sum to the lord and promises to do all the work he ought to do in return for the land. Then the clerk writes it down, so that everyone will know who has the land now. Two men have died since the last court, and the question of who is to have their lands has to be decided. One of them, old William the shepherd, was a villein who held a good deal of land, in return for which he did work every week for the lord. William has left a son, Roger, and now twelve neighbours say that Roger is over twenty-one and that he ought to have the land. But first of all he has to give the lord a chestnut-coloured horse. This payment to the lord is called a *heriot*.

Walter Mustard comes and accuses Simon le Fox of moving the boundary stone between one of his strips and one of Walter's in the East Field, so as to take a bit of Walter's land. This is just the kind of thing Simon would do, but as he was clever enough to do it when no one saw, there are no witnesses, and so he gets off.

Bernard, son of Roger, is accused of killing one of the lord's pigs. While the lord's swineherd was keeping pigs in the woods, Bernard came by carrying a bow of yew and three arrows. He shot one of the arrows from the bow and it pierced the heart of a two-year-old black pig, worth six shillings. Bernard says he was nowhere near the wood and brings witnesses, and asks to have a jury of twelve men to make enquiry. When he has paid sixpence this is allowed, and the jury is to report to the next court.

Rose Newman is fined sixpence for letting her sheep get in the corn. Agnes More is told to clean out her ditch properly. Sabina Tampum is in trouble because she took more brushwood from the common than she should, but she is pardoned because she is so poor. Hugh is fined sixpence for coming late to reap the corn. Margaret, a widow, complains about her neighbour's pigs She says that one afternoon they broke into her garden and rooted up all her beans and cabbages. But she has no witnesses to back her up and everyone agrees that the pigs did not break in, so Margaret is fined sixpence.

The last case is brought by the bailiff against Nicholas Grene, that he has had a suspicious stranger living in his house. It is ordered that the stranger must join a tithing or else leave the village. Can you see why they make the stranger join a tithing? The head men of the tithings ought to have reported this matter, so they are fined threepence eacn for forgetting it.

This ends the business of the court and people begin to go home. Some stop to pay fines, but most people leave their fines till later. While the clerk looks over the roll, adding a word or a figure here and there while he re-members, the steward goes through the cases with the bailiff, and they make a list of the fines and orders to be carried out. The bailiff will have a lot of work to do now If someone will not pay his fine, the bailiff has to seize some of his animals and keep them until he does pay.

Then he has to see that all the orders of the court are carried out, and keep a careful account of all the money he collects.

The clerk is now packing up his rolls. The steward is tired, for there has been an extra lot of business. He has to hold another court in three weeks' time, but he says he is going to have a good day's hunting in between and forget all about the quarrelsome villagers and their disputes.

The villagers do not forget about it all. They go home to supper and talk about everything they have decided that day. Can you imagine what they will be saying? Some people think that Margaret was telling the truth and some say she was lying. Some say that Thomas's fish was rotten and some that it was not. Some think that Adam Doget was the thief and some that he is innocent. Some people say how difficult it is to find out the truth! It is very difficult to prove who has done something unless there are witnesses who saw it happen, and even then you can't always trust witnesses when they are friends. So the villagers very often order someone they suspect to find six more people who will come and swear that they believe he is telling the truth. And sometimes the court chooses twelve men in the village to be a jury and say who they think is in the right.

Do you think these are good ways of trying to find out the truth? The village of Westwood has to manage most of its own affairs and it is very important to make people keep the rules and to find out the truth about those who break them.

HOW DO WE KNOW?

How do we know all this about the village of Westwood 650 years ago? How do we know this book is true? This is the really important question because *what matters most is to find out the truth about things*.

PICTURES. First of all, we know a good deal because men drew pictures of what they saw, just as we do. These men were generally monks who watched people working in the fields round their monasteries, and then drew pictures in the books they were copying, very often in the margins. They didn't always make good pictures—any more than we do—but even a bad drawing by a monk who saw these people with his own eyes probably tells us the truth better than an imaginary picture made today. Some monks drew splendidly, and this book is full of their pictures. A lot of them come from two big books of Psalms which the monks decorated with a great many pictures. They are called the *Luttrell Psalter* and *Queen Mary's Psalter*, and today you can see them in the British Museum in London.

COURT ROLLS. You remember how the clerk wrote down all that happened in the manor court on a great roll? Many of these rolls have been kept safe for six hundred years or more, and now we can read in them reports of everything that happened in many different villages. Of course it is difficult sometimes to puzzle out the handwriting, but it is very exciting to find out what happened so long ago. All the stories in this book come from these court rolls.

ACCOUNT ROLLS. In the same way some of the rolls in which the steward did his accounts to show the lord of the manor have been kept. These tell us about wages, prices and other money matters.

CUSTUMALS. There were so many rules about what the villeins had to do for the lord, and what the lord had to give them, that in many villages, to help their memories, they wrote down these rules or customs in a document called a *custumal*. This is very lucky for us because we can find out from these about the work of the villagers, their rents and their rights.

WILLS. Then, as now, people made wills, and the lists they made in these of the property they wished to leave to others tell us a good deal

83

about their houses, both outside and inside. Not many villeins, however, made wills, because all their property was supposed to belong to their lord.

RECORDS MADE SIX HUNDRED YEARS AGO

This is how men who wrote about *husbandry* described some of the important jobs in the village :

THE GOOD PLOUGHMAN should drive the yoked oxen evenly, neither smiting, pricking nor grieving them. He should not be melancholy or wrathful, but cheerful, jocund and full of song, that by his melody and song the oxen may rejoice in their labour. He should bring *fodder* with his own hands, he should love his oxen and sleep with them at night, tickling and combing and rubbing them with straw.

THE WAGGONER ought to know his trade, to keep the horses and curry them, and to load and carry without danger to his horses, that they may not be overworked, and he must know how to mend his harness. Each waggoner should sleep every night with his horses and keep such guard as he shall wish.

THE COWHERD ought to be skilful, knowing his business and keeping his cows well, and foster the calves well. And he must see that he has fine bulls and large.

THE GOOD SHEPHERD should be watchful and kindly, so that the sheep be not tormented by his wrath, but crop their pasture in peace and joyfulness. It is a token of the shepherd's kindliness if the sheep be not scattered abroad but browse round him in a company. Let him have a good barkable dog, and lie nightly with his flock. Let him not suffer them to feed in miry places or bogs, nor to browse unwholesome herbs.

THE DAIRYMAID ought to be faithful and keep herself clean and ought to know well how to make cheese. She ought to help to winnow the corn when she can be present, and she ought to take care of the geese and hens.

WALTER OF HENLEY'S RULES FOR LOOKING AFTER OXEN

The oxen should each have three sheaves and a half in the week, and in the summer, grass. Keep them so that they have enough food to do their work. Do not let fodder be given them in too great quantity lest they lie down and blow upon it with their nostrils and will not eat it because it is dirty. Wash the beasts and comb them when dry. Rub them down twice daily with a wisp of straw that they may the more lovingly lick themselves.

A PIECE FROM A CHRISTMAS PLAY

(This was written down much later, but perhaps the Christmas Play at Westwood was like this.)

Enter FATHER CHRISTMAS :

      In comes I, old Father Christmas,
      Welcome or welcome not,
      I hope old Father Christmas
      Will never be forgot,
      As Christmas comes but once a year
      And when it comes it brings good cheer.

Enter ST. GEORGE :

      In comes I St. George, the man of courage bold.
      With my broad axe and sword I won three crowns of gold.
      I fought the Fiery Dragon and drove him to the slaughter.
      I won the beautiest queen, the King of Egypt's daughter.
      Then where's the man that dares to bid me stand ?
      I'll cut him down with my courageous hand.
      I'll cut him, I'll hew him
      As small as flies
      And send him to Satan
      To make mincepies.

Enter TURKISH KNIGHT :

      Here comes I the Turkish Knight,
      I come from Turkey's land to fight,
      To fight St. George and all his men
      Before I do return again.

Then they fight until the Turkish Knight falls to the ground.

THINGS TO DO

THE VILLAGE AND THE PEOPLE

1. Paint your own picture of what you think the village of Westwood looked like, using the plan and description of the village to help you. Decide, first of all, whether to paint it in spring, summer, autumn or winter.

2. Write down the chief differences between your house and that of a villein 650 years ago.

3. Dress some dolls like the different villagers. Remember that most of their clothes were woollen and none were made of cotton.

4. Find out all you can about spinning and weaving. You can learn to spin and weave yourself, but first you should make your own loom.

5. Write a conversation between the women in the picture on page 16.

6. Explain why the following things were important to the villagers : *wood, water, salt, wool, leather.*

THE LORD AND THE MANOR HOUSE

1. Make up a conversation between Sir William and his steward about village affairs.

2. Paint a picture of the inside of the manor hall when a feast is going on.

3. Try to find and read some of the ballads the minstrels might have sung in the hall—e.g. ballads of Robin Hood.

4. Write a story about Sir William out hunting.

WORK

1. Make a Calendar of Work with a picture for each month showing what work the villagers were doing then in Westwood.

2. What would a farmer think today about having his land scattered in strips ? Imagine a conversation between John the Villein and a farmer today.

3. Make a frieze to show all the different things the people of Westwood had to do before they could have bread to eat.

4. Paint a picture of the inside of the blacksmith's forge.

5. Make a book on Farming 650 Years Ago and Today. You can collect pictures of farm machinery today and draw your own of the implements used in Westwood. Then arrange them opposite each other and write notes on the differences.

6. Write a song about spring or autumn in Westwood.

FESTIVALS

1. Go and explore your parish church. Find out when it was built. Is it older or newer than the church at Westwood ? Find out if it has any of these in it : *a nave, a chancel, a belfry, a north aisle, a south aisle, transepts, wall-paintings, stained glass windows, ancient tombs.*

2. Get a calendar and find out all the dates of the festivals mentioned in this book. Then make your own calendar of Village Festivals with a picture for each.

3. Explain how we get our word " holiday." Compare our ways of spending holidays with those of the people of Westwood.

4. How many of the games mentioned in this section can you play ? Imagine you are talking to one of the children in Westwood. Tell him (or her) as much as you can about your games.

THE MANOR COURT

1. Explain what the following people had to do in the village : *Reeve, bailiff, steward, aletaster, head tithingman, hayward, constable.*

2. How did the people of Westwood make sure that the lawbreakers were caught and brought to court ?

3. Paint a picture to illustrate the story of Keeper John and Geoffrey of the Moor on page 71.

SUGGESTIONS FOR THINGS TO DO IN A GROUP

1. Make a model of the village of Westwood.

2. Plan an exhibition to show the differences between farming then and now. You can show the differences by models of farm tools and by pictures.

3. Make a play about the village of Westwood, or act a scene in the manor court.

4. Plan and act either a Christmas or a May Day festival. You can have a play in it like the one about St. George, the Turkish Knight and the Dragon.

5. Make some puppet figures of the people of Westwood and make up a play to act with them. (Or you could make puppets of St. George, the Turkish Knight and the Dragon).

GLOSSARY

This is a list of special words. If the word you want to know is not here, look in your dictionary.

arable : ploughed land on which corn and other crops are grown.

Ave : Latin word used in a prayer to the Virgin Mary beginning " Hail Mary !"

bailiff : man who manages the lord of the manor's farming.

beadle : officer of the manor court.

belfrey : tower with a big bell in it.

buck : male deer.

bullock : young ox.

buttery : larder for bread, butter, ale, etc.

capon : cockerel for eating.

cauldron : iron pot for cooking, usually on three legs.

chaff : dry husks (or shells) left when grains of corn have been removed.

chancel : east end of a church, containing the altar.

coulter : knife on a plough which cuts the earth before the *share* slices it and the *mouldboard* turns it over.

crane : large bird with long legs and neck, found in watery places.

custard apple : special kind of apple.

custumal : list of rules or customs of the manor.

demesne : land belonging to the lord of the manor.

distaff : forked stick on which wool is wound before it is spun into twisted thread with a *spindle* (or spinning top).

falconer : man who looks after the lord's hawks.

fallow : land left without a crop so that it shall recover its goodness.

flail : jointed stick for beating corn out of its husks (or shells).

fleece : wool clipped off a sheep all in one piece.

fodder : food (grass, hay, etc.) for animals.

gilly-flower : wallflower or perhaps scented stocks.

girdle : cord tied round the waist.

grindstone : large round stone used for sharpening knives or grinding corn into flour.
goblet : drinking-cup.

harrow : machine with teeth which is dragged over the ground after ploughing.
hayward : man who guards the hay and corn fields.
hemp : tough thread got from nettles and other plants.
heriot : payment made to lord for permission to have your father's land when he is dead.
heron : tall bird with long neck and legs often seen fishing in rivers, etc.
hopper : basket.
hose : stockings.
hue and cry : chase after a thief.
husbandry : the art of looking after your land and animals as described for the medieval village by Walter of Henley.

louvre : smoke-hole in the roof instead of a chimney.
to low : to moo.

marl : earth which is a mixture of clay and lime.
mazer : big bowl used for drinking at feasts.
mead : meadow.
minstrel : man who plays a musical instrument and sings.
mouldboard : see *coulter.*
mummer : village actor disguised to play a part in the revels.

nave : main part of a church where the congregation usually sits.

parchment : skin scraped smooth and prepared for writing on.
pedlar : a man who travelled around on foot, selling small articles which he carried in his pack.
pewter : metal used for plates, mugs, etc., made from a mixture of tin and lead.
plover : bird (otherwise called lapwing, peewit) found usually on moors or hills.
pottage : soup with vegetables or meat in it.
pound : small enclosure in which stray animals are put till they are claimed.

quill pen : one made from a feather.

reeve : villager chosen by the rest to look after their affairs with the
   lord.

Sanctus : Latin word meaning Holy.
screens, the : passage at the end of the hall in the manor house.
scythe : long-handled tool with a sharp, curved blade for cutting hay.
share : see *coulter*.
sheep-shearing : cutting wool off sheep.
sickle : short-handled tool with a sharp, crescent-shaped blade for
   cutting corn.
spindle : see *distaff*.
solar : sun-parlour in the manor house.
steward : overseer of all the lord of the manor's bailiffs.

to tan : to make skins into leather fit for shoes or saddles, etc.
to thresh : to beat the corn out of the husks with *flails*.
tithe : one-tenth of the crops given to the Church and stored by the
   priest in the *tithe-barn*.
tithing : group of ten men each of whom, and especially the head or
   tithingman, has to see that all the rest keep the law.
trencher : wooden plate, or piece of bread used as a plate.
trestle-table : table consisting of a long board laid on movable sets
   of legs.
turnspit : boy who turns the roasting meat on the spit.

venison : meat of deer.
villein : labourer who works on the lord of the manor's land and
   receives land from the lord in return.

wattle and daub wall : made of thin wooden lattice plastered over
   thick with a clay mixture.
wimple : linen cloth which women wind round head and chin.
winnow : to separate grain from chaff.

yoke, to : to harness. The yoke is the collar which is put on the oxen.